KU-432-761

From Fail to Win!
Learning from Bad Ideas

TRANSPORT

Neil Morris

www.raintreepublishers.co.uk
Visit our website to find out more information about Raintree books.

To order:
☎ Phone 0845 6044371
🖨 Fax +44 (0) 1865 312263
💻 Email myorders@raintreepublishers.co.uk

Customers from outside the UK please telephone +44 1865 312262

Raintree is an imprint of Capstone Global Library Limited, a company incorporated in England and Wales having its registered office at 7 Pilgrim Street, London, EC4V 6LB – Registered company number: 6695582

Text © Capstone Global Library Limited 2011
First published in hardback in 2011
The moral rights of the proprietor have been asserted.

All rights reserved. No part of this publication may be reproduced in any form or by any means (including photocopying or storing it in any medium by electronic means and whether or not transiently or incidentally to some other use of this publication) without the written permission of the copyright owner, except in accordance with the provisions of the Copyright, Designs and Patents Act 1988 or under the terms of a licence issued by the Copyright Licensing Agency, Saffron House, 6–10 Kirby Street, London EC1N 8TS (www.cla.co.uk). Applications for the copyright owner's written permission should be addressed to the publisher.

Edited by Andrew Farrow and Vaarunika Dharmapala
Designed by Richard Parker
Original illustrations © Capstone Global Library Ltd 2011
Illustrated by Jeff Edwards
Picture research by Mica Brancic
Originated by Capstone Global Library Ltd
Printed and bound in China by South China Printing Company Ltd

ISBN 978 1 406 21766 7 (hardback)
14 13 12 11 10
10 9 8 7 6 5 4 3 2 1

British Library Cataloguing in Publication Data
Morris, Neil.
From fail to win : learning from bad ideas.
Transport.
388-dc22
A full catalogue record for this book is available from the British Library.

Acknowledgements
We would like to thank the following for permission to reproduce photographs: Alamy pp. 11 (© Mark Scheuern), 28 (© The Print Collector); Corbis pp. 10 (© Bettmann), 20 (© Jim Sugar), 23 (Sygma/© Christian Simonpietri), 29 (© Bettmann), 32 (Roger Ressmeyer/© NASA), 34 (© Bettmann), 36 (© Bettmann), 37 (© Hulton-Deutsch Collection), 39, 41 (© Bettmann), 43 (© Ralph White), 49 (Sygma/© Patrick Durand); Getty Images pp. 5 (Topical Press Agency), 6 (© 2006 David Levenson), 8 (Time Life Pictures/Ed Clark), 14 (Slim Aarons), 15 (Science & Society Picture Library), 16 (Time Life Pictures/Mansell), 18 (Time & Life Pictures/Pierre Boulat), 19 (Phil Cole), 24 (Keystone/Hulton Archive), 27 (Science & Society Picture Library/Science Museum), 30 (MPI), 40 (Lambert), 45 (Davison & Associates Ltd/Fr.fm Browne SJ Collection); Mary Evans Picture Library p. 44 (Onslow Auctions Limited); NASA p. 31; Rex Features pp. 12 (Terrafugia/Ben Schweighart), 48.

Cover photograph of Lincoln Beachey's airship, June 1910, reproduced with permission of Corbis (ClassicStock/© H. Armstrong Roberts).

We would like to thank Ian Graham for his invaluable help in the preparation of this book.

Every effort has been made to contact copyright holders of material reproduced in this book. Any omissions will be rectified in subsequent printings if notice is given to the publisher.

Disclaimer
All the Internet addresses (URLs) given in this book were valid at the time of going to press. However, due to the dynamic nature of the Internet, some addresses may have changed, or sites may have changed or ceased to exist since publication. While the author and publisher regret any inconvenience this may cause readers, no responsibility for any such changes can be accepted by either the author or the publisher.

Leabharlanna Dhún Laoghaire · Ráth An Dúin

Contents

Any words appearing in the text in bold, **like this**, are explained in the glossary

Lessons learned

Technology has come a long way since the **Industrial Revolution** of the 18th and 19th centuries, making transport a pleasure instead of a pain. Most of today's forms of transport are fast, convenient, and comfortable. People travel all over the world without giving it much thought. A huge network of transport routes covers the globe on the ground, over water, and in the air. Astronauts even leave our planet and travel through space. Individual inventors have shown courage and **enterprise** by following their dreams and trying to make things work. Unfortunately they did not always succeed. Those who try new things sometimes fail, especially when the new idea is a moving vehicle. However, others are often able to build on these failures and succeed.

From Cugnot to Sinclair

The earliest failure in this book was the steam cart invented by Nicolas-Joseph Cugnot in 1769. This invention has been called the world's first automobile, and though it was not successful, its failings showed others the way forward. Steam cars had a period of great success, before the water boiler was overtaken by the petrol engine. Today, engineers are looking at ways to replace petrol, and there are sure to be more mistakes along the way. The Sinclair C5 was such a mistake.

A white elephant?

Many of the failures listed in this book, such as Concorde and the Hercules flying boat, have been called "white elephants". This term means a useless possession that is expensive to maintain and impossible to sell. The phrase apparently comes from the story that the King of Siam gave a rare white elephant to a courtier who annoyed him. The king did this knowing that the animal would be costly to keep and could not be put to any practical use.

Newspaper reports in 1950 called the Bristol Brabazon luxury airliner (see page 21) a white elephant. Here, we can compare it with a much smaller aircraft of the time.

Disasters

Some failures end in disaster and loss of life. In the case of the *Apollo* spacecraft fire, the death of three astronauts led to greater safety for those who came after them. The famous *Titanic* disaster led to a number of measures that improved the safety of ocean liners. A single accident not only killed many passengers in the *Hindenburg* airship but also finished off an entire industry.

From fail to win

This book contains 12 examples of failures, ranked from 12 to 1. Some were more important than others in their impact and effect on the future. Comparing one failure with another is not an exact science, so the order in which the projects are ranked is a matter of opinion.

Sinclair C5  No.12

The Sinclair C5 was an electric car developed by the British inventor Clive Sinclair. Launched in 1985, this small three-wheeler was powered by an electric battery. The driver could add power by pedalling, giving a top speed of 24 kilometres (15 miles) per hour.

During the 1970s Sinclair made his name in miniature electronics, including the world's first pocket calculator, the first digital wristwatch, and a tiny television set. In 1980, in the early days of home computers, Sinclair's company offered a small version called a microcomputer. Customers could even buy the microcomputer in kit form and assemble it themselves.

Clive Sinclair launches his C5 electric car in 1985.

FAIL!

Small is better

Sinclair wanted to make a one-person vehicle that was eco-friendly and could be driven by anyone. He kept the speed down, so that C5 owners would not need a driving licence. The driver steered by moving handles beside the driving seat.

Safety concerns

The electric battery drove a small engine, made by a company that also made motors for washing machines and submarine torpedoes. The battery supplied power for up to 32 kilometres (20 miles), and there was space for a spare battery on the vehicle.

The C5 received a very poor reception. Some experts thought that the vehicle was unsafe and impractical, especially in the cold, wet British climate. They thought that drivers would be very vulnerable in city traffic, especially because the car and the driver were so low, and that there could be serious injuries in the case of a collision. The basic C5 did not have direction indicators, wing mirrors, or a horn, all of which had to be bought as extras.

What was learned?

In the 1980s very few drivers were interested in eco-friendly cars. Petrol was still considered to be the most obvious energy source. Things have now changed and, since 2000, several small eco-friendly cars have been launched. Some have proved successful. Major car manufacturers have also done much more work on electric vehicles. They have learned from some of Sinclair's mistakes. They know that people who are interested in an eco-friendly car still want one that is practical and fashionable. People want to drive a fully enclosed car, they want room for at least two people, and they want to be able to travel faster than was possible in the C5.

The VW electric car

Volkswagen presented its new E-Up 3-person electric-battery car at the Frankfurt Motor Show in 2009. Its battery gives it a range of 130 kilometres (80 miles), and the car's top speed is 135 kilometres (84 miles) per hour! Volkswagen says it is easy to recharge the E-Up, and it is also ultra-compact. It is just 3.2 metres (10.5 feet) long and 1.56 metres (5.1 feet) wide. That compares well with the C5's 1.8 metres (6 feet) by 0.8 metres (2.6 feet).

A jet pack, or rocket belt, is a small personal flying device. Several versions have been built since the 1960s, and some have worked. However, none has succeeded in flying for much longer than half a minute, which is a big failing.

FAIL!

Many people still see the jet pack as part of their vision of future transport. They want to put on a pack and fly over busy roads and traffic jams. In this picture, you can see Harold Graham, an engineer from the Bell Aircraft Corporation, demonstrating how their jet pack works.

Novel idea

The Bell Aircraft Corporation is best known for developing the Bell X-1, the aircraft that first broke the sound barrier in 1947 (see page 19). Fifteen years later, Bell demonstrated its rocket belt – a 57-kilogram (125-pound) backpack that was worn by a pilot, who could then fly for distances up to about 250 metres (820 feet). However, there were major problems. The jet pack could fly for only a very short time, it was difficult to control and steer, and its fuel was very dangerous. These problems made it an impractical proposition.

How does it work?

A jet pack is powered by superheated water vapour. The pilot wears a device with three gas cylinders, one of nitrogen and two of hydrogen peroxide. These gases produce a mixture of superheated steam and oxygen that blasts out through two nozzles to provide **thrust**. The pilot, who wears insulating clothes as protection against the extreme heat, uses hand-operated steering controls. A timer tells the pilot when 15 seconds have passed, so that he can make sure he is in a safe position to land.

What was learned?

Several companies and individuals are working on improved jet packs. Even so, the problems of limited flying time, danger of the method of **propulsion**, and difficulty in steering remain. Perhaps inventors will overcome these difficulties, but the jet pack may ultimately remain a form of futuristic entertainment rather than a genuine means of travel.

James Bond zooms off

In the 1965 film *Thunderball*, James Bond strapped on a jet pack and blasted off in a huge swirl of dust. In fact, the pilot was a stunt man and the accompanying sound was made by a fire extinguisher. The jet pack itself made an unpleasant high-pitched screech. Rocket belts were also used to entertain crowds at the 1967 American Football Super Bowl and the opening ceremony of the 1984 Olympic Games, both in Los Angeles.

The successful MMU

The exception to this might be in the case of space travel. The National **Aeronautics** and Space Administration's (NASA) Manned Maneuvering Unit (MMU) was used successfully on three space shuttle missions in 1984. It allowed astronauts to move in space outside the spacecraft. On the third mission, astronauts used the MMU to capture two communication satellites and take them to their shuttle. The MMU was powered by high-pressure nitrogen and could power space flight for up to six hours. The astronaut used hand controls to steer. It seems this was easier in the weightlessness of space than in Earth's **atmosphere**.

The Mizar

In 1971 the American engineer Henry Smolinski set up a company called Advanced Vehicle Engineers to build a flying car. The result was the Mizar, which had the rear end of an aircraft attached to a Ford Pinto car. Although the plane took off a few times, the idea never did. The project ended in tragedy.

FAIL!

Henry Smolinski called his flying plane the Mizar after a star in the constellation of the Great Bear.

Early developments

Inventors started work on a flying car shortly after the introduction of cars and planes. The first was American aviator Glenn Curtiss, who built his three-winged aluminium Autoplane in 1917. It hopped off the ground but never really took off. Twenty years later, Waldo Waterman designed a high-wing **monoplane** with detachable wings that did fly. In 1949, the American engineer Moulton Taylor came up with his Aerocar. In this model the wings and tail folded away behind the vehicle. These were promising developments, but none of the flying cars went into production.

The engineer Moulton Taylor built six Aerocars between 1949 and 1960. The Aerocar pictured here is the only one still able to be flown.

Advanced Vehicle Engineers

By 1973 Smolinski had finished building two Mizar **prototypes** and had started to build three more. The Mizar had two engines, one for the car and another for the plane. It used both for take-off, and once airborne, the car engine was switched off. When landing, the car brakes could stop the plane in just 160 metres (525 feet). Then the car was supposed to be unbolted from the airframe and driven away from the airfield. Smolinski planned to put the Mizar into full production in 1974, but then disaster struck. On a test flight in California on 11 September 1973, one of the wing struts came away from the car. The plane crashed, killing both Smolinski and his pilot, Harold Blake. That was the end of the Mizar project.

Skymaster and Pinto

The plane used in the Mizar was the US twin-engine Skymaster utility aircraft. It first flew in 1961, and nearly 3,000 of them were built between 1963 and 1982. Unlike the aircraft, the Pinto car was a failure, although 3.1 million were produced in the United States in the 1970s. It was said that the Pinto's rear end was not strong enough and the fuel tank was easily damaged if the car was hit from behind. This was thought to have caused explosions and fires. Pressure from motorists caused the US National Highway Traffic Safety Administration to suggest that Ford recall the cars for modification.

What was learned?

Part of the problem with the Mizar was deciding whether a flying car is a car that can fly or a plane that can drive. Some aviation experts call flying cars "roadable aircraft", showing that they believe they are really planes. The Mizar disaster has led developers to try to make the craft one piece, rather than two pieces that may come apart. According to a report in the *New York Times* in 2009, 11 companies are currently developing their own versions. Will any of them succeed? Or have we learned that trying to combine two forms of transport, such as a car and a plane, simply doesn't work? Only time will tell.

Terrafugia Transition

The Terrafugia Transition is a new roadable aircraft, or "dual-purpose vehicle", developed by a group of aeronautical engineers in Massachusetts, USA. It is designed with folding wings that transform it from a two-seater car into a plane in less than 30 seconds.

In 2009 the Terrafugia Transition had several successful test flights.

Ford Nucleon

In the 1950s people started talking about the "Atomic Age". Many believed that nuclear power was the energy source of the future. Car manufacturers looked at replacing the petrol engine with a nuclear **reactor**, and in 1958 the Ford Motor Company unveiled its new concept car: the Nucleon. This futuristic Ford was nuclear-powered.

The Atomic Age

After World War II, people involved in energy production were interested in nuclear power. An experimental reactor was used to generate electricity in Idaho, USA, in 1951. Five years later, the world's first full-scale commercial nuclear plant opened at Sellafield, in the United Kingdom. The main vehicle that used nuclear reactors was the submarine. The first such vessel – USS *Nautilus* – was launched in 1954, and its early voyages broke all records for time and distance travelled underwater.

How did it work?

The Nucleon had its own miniature reactor containing **radioactive** uranium. Inside, a chain reaction of splitting **nuclei** gave off the heat needed to boil water which created high-pressure steam. The steam drove a turbine, which turned the wheels of the car. Engineers thought that a Nucleon would be able to travel for about 8,000 kilometres (5,000 miles) before the core of the reactor needed recharging. That was because it takes very little uranium to produce an enormous amount of power. The car just needed nuclear stations instead of petrol stations.

The Nucleon according to Ford:

"Cars such as the Nucleon illustrate the extent to which research into the future was conducted at Ford, and demonstrate the designer's unwillingness to admit that a thing cannot be done simply because it has not been done."

Ford media website 2010

FAIL!

This photograph shows William Ford with a model of the Nucleon. The nuclear-powered car never got beyond the model stage, despite a lot of publicity.

Submarine success

Small nuclear reactors can be well contained in ships, and nuclear-powered submarines have been a great success. Even so, there have been some incidents, and environmentalists are concerned that any major accident could be harmful to the oceans. There is also the question of how to dispose of used nuclear fuel safely. This would have been a constant problem with the Ford Nucleon.

What was learned?

The main problem with the Nucleon was safety. The Ford designers had created a sealed-off cockpit for the driver and passengers, and this was as far away from the reactor as possible. However, nuclear reactions give off radiation, which is extremely harmful to people. That is why reactors in nuclear power stations are sealed in metres of thick concrete, which is not possible in a car. The chain reactions also have to be carefully controlled, to avoid producing an explosion. Any nuclear explosion, even from a tiny reactor, is devastating and causes enormous damage and loss of life. With our present-day knowledge of nuclear dangers, the very notion of the Nucleon seems ridiculous.

Langley's Aerodrome

Question: who invented, built, and flew the world's first power-driven aeroplane? Answer: Wilbur and Orville Wright, on 17 December 1903 in North Carolina, USA. The answer might have been different, however, if things had not gone wrong just nine days earlier for another US air pioneer named Samuel Langley. His powered aircraft failed, and the rest is history.

Powered flight

Samuel Langley was a remarkable man. As well as being an inventor and a pioneer of aviation, he was a mathematician, physicist, and astronomer. He was also secretary of the Smithsonian Institution, a famous organization that promotes science, education, and culture. He started building powered model aeroplanes in 1892. Seven years later, Wilbur Wright wrote to Langley asking for information on aeronautical research. A colleague at the Smithsonian sent a package of papers, including Langley's *Experiments in Aerodynamics*. The Wright brothers later wrote that this material gave them a "good understanding of the nature of the problem of flying".

Plane or airfield?

Today we use the word *aerodrome* to mean an airfield. The word comes from Greek and means "air running or course". Langley first used it in 1891 as a name for a model aeroplane. The word took on its modern meaning in 1908.

The Aerodrome had separate front and rear wings. The pilot sat on the framework between them.

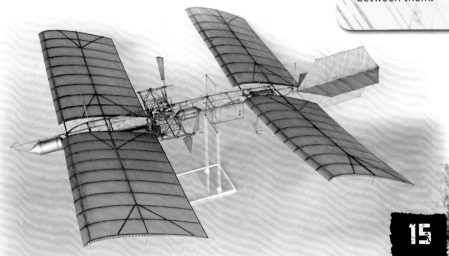

Power and launch

In 1903 Langley built a full-scale version of his Aerodrome. Engineer Charles Manly, who had worked on the engine, agreed to be test pilot. The plane needed a catapult for launching. This would have ruled the Aerodrome out as the first self-powered manned flying machine, even if it had been successful. It was this launch catapult that proved to be the big problem.

In October 1903 the plane was put together on a specially built houseboat on the Potomac River in Virginia. When it was launched, the catapult snagged the aircraft, which fell into the river. The same thing happened on the next attempt in December. This time Manly was trapped in the wreckage, but managed to cut himself free.

A disappointed man

"Nobody came closer to producing an aeroplane capable of powered, sustained flight without actually achieving this aim ... Today Langley's Aerodrome is acknowledged to have been the first man-carrying aeroplane capable of flight."

Michael Taylor,
A Photographic History of Flight,
2005

FAIL!

The Aerodrome is ready for launch on top of a houseboat. Fortunately, rescue boats are also at the ready.

What was learned?

Samuel Langley was ridiculed by the press and gave up his aviation career. He died in 1906, but eight years later, the famous air pioneer Glenn Curtiss modified the Aerodrome and made a few short flights in it. Like many other flying machines of the time and the next few decades, Langley's aircraft had strengths and weaknesses. The biggest weakness was the tricky launching system. Air pioneers learned from all their rivals' successes and failures, and in that way Langley's efforts helped to advance powered flight.

The first successful powered flight

Nine days after the first Aerodrome failure, Wilbur Wright wrote in a letter: "I see that Langley has had his fling, and failed. It seems to be our turn to throw now, and I wonder what our luck will be".

On 17 December 1903, his brother Orville piloted the Flyer plane for its first flight. He was airborne for 12 seconds and flew 36 metres (118 feet). The fourth and final attempt was the most successful. Wilbur flew for 59 seconds and covered 260 metres (853 feet).

	Langley Aerodrome	Wright Flyer
Wingspan (metres/feet)	14.8 (48.5)	12.3 (40.3)
Length (metres/feet)	16.0 (52.4)	6.4 (20.9)
Height (metres/feet)	3.5 (11.4)	2.8 (9.1)
Weight (kilograms/ pounds)	274 (604)	274 (604)
Engine power (horse power)	52	12

This table shows you how the failed and successful planes compared.

Concorde

The Aérospatiale-BAC Concorde was a **supersonic** passenger aircraft that flew for more than 25 years. Many people saw it as a symbol of advanced technology and state-of-the-art design. However, Concorde was expensive to build and fly, and it was never a financial success.

Early development

During the 1950s, scientists in the United Kingdom, France, the United States, and the **USSR** became interested in getting aircraft to fly as fast as possible, to cut journey times. They all worked on developing supersonic aircraft. The United Kingdom set up a Supersonic Transport Aircraft Committee in 1956. Six years later the British Aircraft Corporation (BAC) and French Aérospatiale decided to join forces on development. In the United States, Boeing Commercial Airplanes worked on a **prototype** for a supersonic Boeing-2707, but the project was eventually cancelled. It was a different story in the USSR, where the Tupolev Tu-144 was developed (see pages 22–25).

This Concorde is parked inside a hangar in France.

Take-off

After seven years' work, the first Concorde took off on a test flight at Toulouse, France, on 2 March 1969. Engineers and pilots spent 5,000 flying hours testing the plane, and Concorde finally began passenger flights in 1976 with British Airways and Air France.

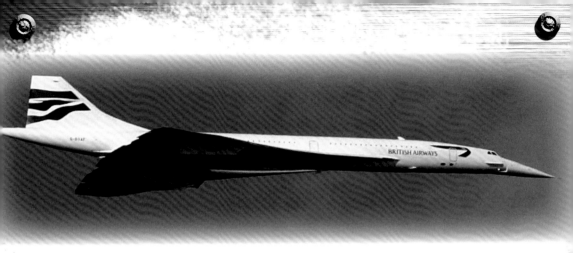

Eventually each airline had seven Concordes, and six more were built as prototypes and non-service planes.

Pluses and minuses

The first scheduled flights were from London to Bahrain and from Paris to Rio de Janeiro. The biggest advantage was speed, since supersonic flight cut the scheduled times enormously. However, there were problems too. At first the United States would not allow Concorde flights at all. Then Washington, DC was cleared for landing, and finally New York. The main issue was noise, and especially the fear of **sonic booms**. Even so, passengers soon realized the value of supersonic speed. The transatlantic flight took about 3 hours, and in 1996 a London to New York record was set at 2 hours and 53 minutes. The airlines also made sure that their sonic booms took place over the ocean, where they disturbed no one. Even though Concorde had advantages, one of its main problems was that tickets were expensive. There were two reasons for this: the operating costs of the planes were very high, and each could only carry 100 passengers.

The first supersonic plane

The Bell X-1 (also see page 8) was the world's first supersonic aircraft. This small American plane was just 9.4 metres (30.8 feet) long, with a wingspan of 8.5 metres (27.8 feet). It flew faster than the speed of sound on 14 October 1947, after being carried into the air by a B-29 bomber plane. Before this, many pilots had been worried about flying faster than sound and "breaking the sound barrier". When planes flew at near-sonic speed, they got very hot and experienced huge **shock waves**.

Fuel consumption

Concorde was a gas-guzzler. It flew less than 6 kilometres (3.7 miles) per passenger per litre of jet fuel. This is a little less than a small business jet, which may fly nearly 7 kilometres (4.3 miles) per passenger per litre. A Boeing 747 jumbo jet can fly more than 38 kilometres (23 miles) per passenger per litre – that is over six times as fuel-efficient as Concorde.

In-flight service on Concorde was luxurious, but passengers did not have nearly as much room as on a jumbo jet.

Coming to an end

By the turn of the 21st century, Concorde's computer systems were no longer state-of-the-art and the aircraft needed an expensive update. At the same time, airlines had grown used to flying jumbo jets, such as the Boeing 747. The big jets were certainly slower, but a 747 could carry more than 500 passengers and was also much quieter.

Paris crash

On 25 July 2000 an Air France Concorde flight bound for New York crashed shortly after take-off in Paris. All 100 passengers and 9 crew were killed, along with 4 people on the ground. The crash was probably caused by a fractured fuel tank, which started an under-wing fire on take-off. The tank had been hit by a strip of metal on the runway, which had fallen from another aircraft and caused one of the Concorde's tyres to explode.

This was the only fatal accident involving a Concorde aircraft, and it led to immediate safety improvements. New linings were added to the fuel tanks, and burst-resistant tyres were fitted. After the modifications, passenger flights started again in November 2001. Less than 18 months later, however, Air France and British Airways announced the end of their Concorde flights. The reasons for this decision were low passenger numbers and rising maintenance costs.

What has been learned?

Today Japanese companies and others are researching the development of a supersonic business jet for the future. Many lessons have been learned from Concorde, but will any company be able to overcome the problems and disadvantages? Airlines have surely learned that passengers are not necessarily happy to pay more simply to travel faster. Many would prefer to travel in more spacious, comfortable seats so that they can relax or work. As for aircraft manufacturers, it is likely that development will concentrate on larger, quieter, more fuel-efficient, and environmentally friendly aircraft.

Unwanted luxury

An earlier airliner designed for the luxury transatlantic market was such a failure that it never even made a scheduled flight. The Bristol Brabazon (also see page 5) was supposed to give wealthy passengers an experience similar to being on an ocean liner. The aircraft was designed with sleeping berths for 80 passengers on night flights, or seats for 150 passengers on daytime flights. It had a dining room, cinema, lounge, and cocktail bar. Despite these luxuries, no airline bought the plane and the single prototype was broken up for scrap in 1953.

Tupolev Tu-144

There have only ever been two **supersonic** passenger planes –
Concorde and the **Soviet** Tupolev Tu-144. The Tu-144 was not
a long-term success. In fact, it lasted for only ten years, between
its first test flight in 1968 and its last passenger flight in 1978
(see table on page 23).

Concorde

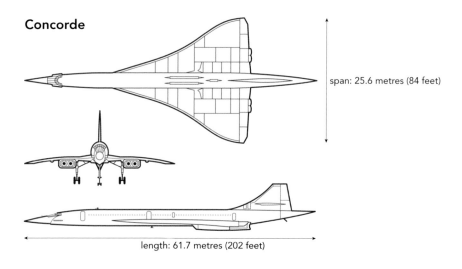

span: 25.6 metres (84 feet)

length: 61.7 metres (202 feet)

Tu-144

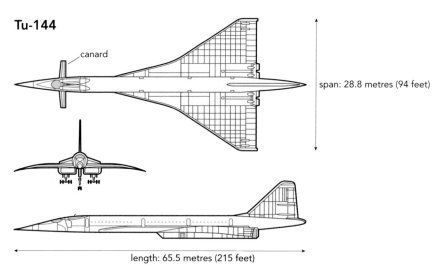

canard

span: 28.8 metres (94 feet)

length: 65.5 metres (215 feet)

Like Concorde, the Tu-144 had large, swept-back wings.
Unlike its rival, later versions of the Soviet plane had a
pair of small wings called canards at the front. These
helped give the plane extra lift at low speed.

Copying to catch up?

During the 1960s the **USSR** and the United States were racing each other to be the first to introduce a supersonic passenger aircraft. The Russians started later, but amazingly they won the race, when their Tu-144 took off on 31 December 1968. It bore a remarkable resemblance to Concorde, which had been started earlier but first flew just over two months later. It was said that Russian spies stole plans from the Aérospatiale company in France. The British press were sure that this was true, and gave the Tu-144 the nickname "Concordski".

Tupolev family

The Tu-144's development was led by the Soviet aircraft designer Aleksey Andreyevich Tupolev (pictured), who went on to help design the Russian Buran space shuttle. He was the son of the famous aircraft pioneer Andrei Nikolayevich Tupolev. Aleksey graduated from the Moscow Aviation Institute in 1949 and became chief designer of the Tupolev Design Bureau in 1963.

	Tupolev Tu-144	Concorde
First flight	31 December 1968	2 March 1969
First supersonic flight	5 June 1969	1 October 1969
First passenger flight	1 November 1977	21 January 1976
Last passenger flight	1 June 1978	24 October 2003

This table shows you how the Tu-144 and Concorde compared.

"Although it bore a close superficial resemblance to Concorde, Russia's Tupolev Tu-144 was both aerodynamically and technologically inferior, and saw only limited service."

Richard Bickers,
A Century of Manned Flight,
1998

Air-show disaster

Four years after its first flight, the Tu-144 was still not in service, as further tests and improvements took place. The Russians decided to show the improved plane off at the Paris air show. On 3 June 1973 crowds of people first watched a Concorde perform perfectly. Then it was the Tu-144's turn. Unfortunately the Russian pilot didn't know a French Mirage jet would photograph his plane from above. When he saw the Mirage close by, he swerved to avoid a collision, then dived steeply. The plane crashed, killing all six crew and eight people on the ground.

Short service

After further modifications, the Tu-144 at last went into service in December 1975, but it carried post and **freight** rather than passengers. Nearly two years later, the first passengers flew on a Tu-144. Only 102 scheduled passenger flights ever took place. On 23 May 1978 a new plane failed and crash-landed on a test flight. Nine days later the Tu–144 flew its last passenger flight.

This photograph shows the terrible aftermath of the 1973 crash of the Tu-144. The official report into the accident blamed the pilot.

Flying Laboratory

In the mid-1990s, old rivalries were forgotten when Russia and the United States decided to test supersonic flight together. Tupolev modified an old Tu-144, and they, NASA, and Boeing turned it into the Tu-144LL Flying Laboratory. It made 27 flights to test the supersonic systems. No airlines appeared to be interested in buying supersonic planes, however, and the project ended in 1999.

What has been learned?

The Tu-160, introduced in 1987, benefited from past experiences with the Tu-144. This supersonic bomber is the largest swing-wing aircraft (with wings that can move to a swept-back position during flight) ever built. There are plans for a Tu-244, another attempt at a supersonic passenger aircraft. This would be bigger, faster, and fly further than the Tu-144. Tupolev are planning a supersonic business jet for a maximum of ten passengers. The table below shows how these two future possibilities compare with the two supersonic planes that have already flown. Perhaps past failure will lead to future success.

	Concorde	Tu-144	Tu-244 (proposed)	Tu-444 (proposed)
First flight	1969	1968	–	–
In service	1976-2003	1975-78	–	–
Length (metres/feet)	61.7 (202)	65.5 (215)	88.7 (291)	36 (118)
Wingspan (metres/feet)	25.6 (84)	28.8 (94)	54.8 (180)	16.2 (53)
Height (metres/feet)	12.2 (40)	12.3 (40.3)	16.9 (55.5)	6.5 (21)
Passengers	100	126	250-320	6-10
Number built	20	17	–	–

The steam engine was invented in Britain in the 1700s. Various versions and improvements were made by Thomas Savery, Thomas Newcomen, and James Watt, who took out his first **patent** on a steam engine in 1769. At the same time, engineers and inventors were dreaming of a "horseless carriage" to transport people. Many thought that steam was the best source of power for this "dream machine", which would be cheaper and cleaner than previous carriages and do away with the need to keep horses.

"The process that led to the invention and marketing of the automobile had its roots in the history of the steam-powered horseless carriage … But the invention of the internal combustion engine rendered even the 'hot' steam car dated".

Richard Sutton,
Motor Mania,
1996

Steaming along

A French military engineer called Nicolas-Joseph Cugnot thought up several inventions while taking part in the Seven Years' War (1756–1763). After returning to Paris in 1763, he concentrated on one of these – an idea for using steam to power a cart or carriage. By 1769 he had made a working model of his first steam cart, replacing the horses at the front with a huge boiler, steam engine, and a single iron-rimmed wheel. The cart had two wheels at the back. This steam cart was the world's first self-propelled road vehicle.

The steam engine drove the front wheel, which was also used to steer the vehicle. One drawback was that the cart had to stop every 10 to 15 minutes, so that the boiler could build up enough steam pressure to drive the engine pistons and therefore the wheels. At full pressure, the carriage had a top speed of little over 3 kilometres (1.8 miles) per hour. Another problem was that the vehicle was unstable.

Cugnot's steam cart of 1770 is still on display in a museum. In this photograph, you can see the two-handed steering handle in front of the driver's bench.

French army generals were very interested in Cugnot's work. They thought that his vehicle could carry heavy loads, such as big guns. The original specification was that it could carry up to 4 tonnes (4.4 tons) and cover 8 kilometres (5 miles) in an hour, but the steam cart never managed this. Tests also showed that it was difficult to drive, which made it less attractive to everyone.

Nicolas-Joseph Cugnot

Cugnot was born in France in 1725. He trained as a military engineer. After the French Revolution of 1789, he spent several years living abroad. Cugnot died in Paris in 1804.

Failing the test

Cugnot's second, improved model was involved in the world's first automobile accident. The vehicle ran out of control and knocked down part of a stone wall (see illustration below). Cugnot designed another model for carrying passengers, but there were reports that it rolled over – a problem common to three-wheelers. The project was abandoned but the French king Louis XV granted Cugnot a generous pension for his inventive work.

Improving the steam car

Other attempts were made to improve the steam car. In the early 20th century, cars made by Francis and Freelan Stanley, known as Stanley Steamers, were very popular. The steamers had four wheels, making them much more stable than Cugnot's cart. Steam was generated in a boiler mounted under the seat, which gave the driver a clear view ahead.

The arrival of petrol

In 1906 a Stanley steam car broke the world land speed record when it reached 203 kilometres (126 miles) per hour at Ormond Beach, Florida, USA. By 1924, however, petrol-engine cars were becoming more efficient, powerful, and were cheaper. In that year, a Stanley steamer sedan cost nearly eight times more than a Model T Ford petrol car. The Stanley company tried to convince customers that petrol engines were unreliable and even dangerous. Despite this campaign, steam eventually lost out to petrol.

What was learned?

Cugnot's steam cart failed, but there is no doubt that later inventors learned from his mistakes. Steam went on to power the **Industrial Revolution** which, in turn, led to new technologies, problems, and solutions. Today, steam has been almost completely replaced by petrol and diesel. We now know that these fuels cause harm to the environment. They may themselves be soon replaced by cars which use **biofuels**, hydrogen fuel cells, and electricity.

The Dymaxion

In 1933 the US inventor and architect Buckminster Fuller unveiled his new Dymaxion car. It could carry 12 passengers and reach a speed of 190 kilometres (120 miles) per hour. The car had a teardrop-shaped, 6.1-metre (20-foot) long body, and three wheels. The single wheel was at the rear, and the powerful Ford V8 engine drove the front two wheels. Unusually, it was the rear wheel that steered the car. At the 1933 Chicago World's Fair the car rolled over, killing the driver, and seriously injuring the two passengers. The Dymaxion was never mass produced.

Here, the Dymaxion is on display at the White House in Washington, DC, USA.

In 1967 the US National **Aeronautics** and Space Administration (NASA) was testing a manned Apollo spacecraft at Cape Canaveral in Florida. Three astronauts, Command Pilot Gus Grissom, Senior Pilot Edward White, and Pilot Roger Chaffee, were in the command module on top of a huge rocket. They were going through a simulated (pretend) launch, getting ready for the real thing planned for a month later. Suddenly disaster struck. The intended launch never took place, and the first manned Apollo mission was held up for 20 months.

Gus Grissom, Edward White, and Roger Chaffee carry out checks in the *Apollo 1* practice module.

Race to the Moon

Yuri Gagarin of the **USSR** had been the first human in space on 12 April 1961. The following month Alan Shepard became the first American in space. Just weeks later US President John F. Kennedy announced a programme to land an astronaut on the Moon before the end of the 1960s. The programme was named Apollo, and NASA worked on designing a spacecraft to carry three astronauts to the Moon in a cone-shaped command module (CM).

Testing the rocket and spacecraft

There were many test launches for the Apollo rocket and spacecraft before the first manned flight attempt. This failed mission was originally called Apollo-Saturn-204. It was later named *Apollo 1*. The aim of the mission was to launch a command and service module (CSM) into space so that it could orbit Earth for up to 14 days.

This is the *Apollo 1* mission patch. Similar badges are often worn by NASA astronauts on their flights.

Disaster strikes

On 27 January 1967, Grissom, White, and Chaffee took their places in the CM and closed the hatch. The astronauts were running through a checklist of pre-launch tests, when they suddenly shouted that there was a fire in the cockpit. There was intense heat and smoke, and 17 seconds later there was silence from the crew. Ground staff rushed to the CM, but the heat and smoke made it difficult to open the inward-opening hatch. Some minutes later, they found they were too late to save the astronauts, whose bodies and spacesuits were badly burned.

JFK's famous words

On 25 May 1961 President John F. Kennedy said in a speech:

"I believe that this nation should commit itself to achieving the goal, before this decade is out, of landing a man on the moon and returning him safely to the Earth. No single space project in this period will be more impressive to mankind, or more important for the long-range exploration of space; and none will be so difficult or expensive to accomplish".

What failed?

The fire was probably caused by a spark from an electrical short circuit somewhere in the 25 kilometres (15.5 miles) of wiring that ran through the CM. It burned fiercely because the **atmosphere** inside the CM was pure oxygen and the cabin pressure was very high. Some of the materials inside the CM were **flammable**, and parts of the crew's nylon spacesuits and seat covers were melted by the heat. The official report on the accident later said the temperature in the cabin reached more than 530 °C (986 °F).

The burned-out inside of the command module shows how intense the heat was.

FAIL!

What was learned?

Everyone knew that in space exploration, safety concerns had to be given top priority. The accident underlined this and led to a number of changes in future CMs:

- Wiring was covered with protective insulation.
- The cabin pressure was lowered for the launch and ascent phases of the mission.

- Flammable materials were replaced with non-flammable ones.
- Nylon spacesuits were replaced with fireproof **fibreglass** fabric.
- An outward-opening hatch was installed.

These changes led directly to the success of the first manned flight of *Apollo 7* and the Moon landing of *Apollo 11* in 1969. The following year, *Apollo 13* experienced an explosion in the service module in space. Lessons learned from the failure of *Apollo 1* helped the astronauts survive the ordeal and return to Earth safely.

As the table below shows, it took only about two years from *Apollo 1* to the first Moon landing.

Apollo no.	Rocket	Commander	Launch date	Mission
1	*Saturn IB*	Gus Grissom	planned for 21 February 1967	Launch pad test
7	*Saturn IB*	Wally Schirra	11 October 1968	Earth orbit
8	*Saturn V*	Frank Borman	21 December 1968	Moon orbit
9	*Saturn V*	Jim McDivitt	3 March 1969	Earth orbit
10	*Saturn V*	Thomas Stafford	18 May 1969	Moon orbit with lunar module
11	*Saturn V*	Neil Armstrong	16 July 1969	Moon landing

Soyuz 1

Three months after the *Apollo 1* disaster, the USSR's *Soyuz 1* spacecraft crash-landed. After orbiting Earth 18 times with a single cosmonaut on board, the spacecraft's parachutes failed. This caused it to hit the ground much too fast. There was an explosion and a fire, and cosmonaut Vladimir Komarov was killed. Improvements were made to the spacecraft and there were many successful missions, but no manned **Soviet** spacecraft landed on the Moon.

"Spruce Goose" No.3

On 2 November 1947 a new flying boat was tested on the calm waters of Los Angeles harbour, in California, USA. The huge H-4 Hercules aircraft had the largest wingspan of any plane ever built. On the third test run, spectators were surprised to see the huge plane speed up and then lift off the water. The Hercules, nicknamed "Spruce Goose", flew for 60 seconds before touching down again. Nobody on board knew that this minute-long flight was to be the plane's only flight ever. The aircraft, which cost millions of dollars to develop, never flew again.

The project to build the H-4 Hercules was the idea of two businessmen. Henry Kaiser ran a shipbuilding company and Howard Hughes was a manufacturer and film producer. In 1942, during World War II, the US government was looking for ways to fly cargo across the Atlantic to Europe. German submarines were sinking US ships, so planes seemed to be the answer. Kaiser and Hughes were given a contract to build three flying boats.

The enormous "Spruce Goose" dwarfs the boats in Los Angeles harbour.

Built of birch

During World War II, aluminium and steel were in short supply because they were needed for military vehicles and weapons. So the Hughes design team decided to build their aeroplane of wood. They developed a new process, called Duramold, which used plastic glue to stick together thin sheets of wood, mainly birch. The laminated wood could be heated and shaped, and the resulting material was light and strong.

When the war ended in 1945, the US government and Henry Kaiser pulled out, so Howard Hughes was left to finish the project on his own. He told a government committee: "The Hercules … is the largest aircraft ever built. It is over five stories tall with a wingspan longer than a football field … Now, I put the sweat of my life into this thing. I have my reputation all rolled up in it and I have stated several times that if it's a failure I'll probably leave this country and never come back".

One and only flight

Journalists called Hughes's plane the "Spruce Goose" (though it was made of birch rather than spruce). Despite the funny name, they must have been impressed by the aircraft's statistics. Howard Hughes himself was at the controls when the plane used its eight engines to fly at 24 metres (78 feet) above the water for about 1.6 kilometres (1 mile). So why did it never fly again?

Why "flying boats"?

Flying boats became popular during the 1930s, when planes could not fly very far without landing and there were few airports. The first aircraft to cross the Atlantic Ocean was a Curtiss NC-4 flying boat in 1919. However, this was far from a non-stop flight. The NC-4 made 8 landings and flew for more than 57 hours over a period of 15 days! These big planes had under-wing floats, so they could land on and take off from water. Passengers were ferried to and from the aircraft by boat.

The mysterious Howard Hughes

Hughes knew there was no longer a need for his enormous plane and that technological advances were being made in other aircraft. He had proved that the Hercules could fly, and perhaps that was enough for him. Nevertheless, he paid a crew to keep the plane in flying condition until he died in 1976. During the last 20 years of his life, Howard Hughes kept out of the public eye. He was still fabulously rich, and mystery surrounded this man who never appeared in public.

What was learned?

From 1983–1988 the H-4 Hercules was displayed next to the *Queen Mary* ocean liner at Long Beach, California, USA. Then it was taken to the Evergreen Aviation Museum in McMinnville, Oregon, USA, where it is still on display. Although the Hercules failed, it was the forerunner of later transport aircraft. Examples are the American Lockheed C-5 Galaxy and the Russian Antonov An-124 (see table on page 37). Both were built of metal, but the "Spruce Goose" had shown that such huge aircraft could fly.

Howard Hughes sits at the controls of the Spruce Goose. It cost him millions of dollars to build.

	Hercules H-4	C-5 Galaxy	Antonov An-124
First flight	1947	1968	1982
Length (metres/feet)	66.7 (218.8)	75.3 (247)	69.0 (226.3)
Wingspan (metres/feet)	97.5 (319.8)	67.9 (222.7)	73.3 (240.4)
Height (metres/feet)	24.2 (79.3)	19.8 (64.9)	20.8 (68.2)
Loaded weight (tonnes/tons)	180 (198.4)	348.8 (384.5)	405 (446.4)
Quantity built	1	131	56

The first flying-boat failure

The maiden flights of some earlier flying boats were less successful. The Italian Caproni Ca-60 was a 100-passenger, 9-wing flying boat with 8 engines. Like the Hercules, only one was ever built. On 4 March 1921 the Ca-60 took off from Lake Maggiore, in Italy, reached a height of 18 metres (59 feet), and then crashed and broke up. The pilot escaped unharmed.

The Caproni flying boat was the largest aeroplane in the world before it was destroyed during its first flight.

Hindenburg

In the early 20th century many people thought that balloons were better than winged aircraft for passenger flight. Large cigar-shaped balloons were powered by propellers, and these gas-filled airships, also called zeppelins or dirigibles, were much more spacious than airliners. However, a single disaster showed how flimsy and dangerous they were.

Taking off

The Zeppelin LZ-129 airship was named the *Hindenburg* after Paul von Hindenburg, president of Germany from 1925 to 1934. The huge airship had an aluminium-alloy framework, with 16 cotton gas-bags fitted between bulkheads and surrounded by a skin of treated cotton. It was built for transatlantic flights, but its first job in 1936 was to fly over Germany, acting as **propaganda** for the Nazi dictator, Adolf Hitler. After this success, the *Hindenburg* flew across the Atlantic to Rio de Janeiro and back.

These are deck layouts inside the *Hindenburg*.

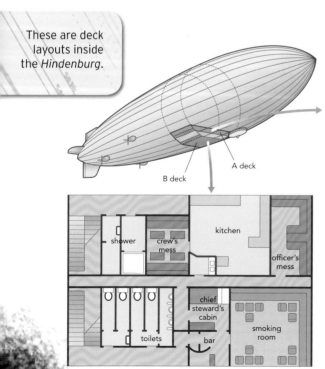

B deck

A deck

B deck floor plan

shower
crew's mess
kitchen
officer's mess
chief steward's cabin
smoking room
toilets
bar

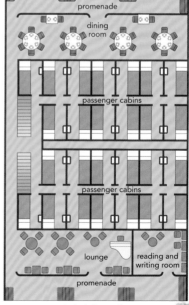

A deck floor plan

promenade
dining room
passenger cabins
passenger cabins
lounge
reading and writing room
promenade

Transatlantic luxury

The *Hindenburg* made a further 6 return trips to Brazil in 1936, plus 10 trips to the United States. On one trip it set a record by completing the return journey in less than two days. The flights were fast and luxurious. The passenger cabins were small, but they had hot showers and there were spacious public areas. These included a dining room, lounge with a grand piano, and library. There were windows along the length of both the upper and lower deck, and passengers praised the facilities and the smooth flight.

Zeppelins

German airships were named after Count Ferdinand von Zeppelin, who originally designed them. Zeppelin trained to be an army officer and visited the United States, where he rode in military balloons. When he retired from the army he turned to **aeronautics**. His first airship, the LZ-1, made its maiden flight in 1900.

This photograph shows passengers enjoying the luxury of the *Hindenburg's* dining room.

Hydrogen versus helium

Airship engineers knew that helium is much safer than hydrogen, because it is not **flammable**. The *Hindenburg* was designed to use helium, but this gas was expensive and available mainly from US gas reserves. The United States had banned the export of helium, because it was needed for its own airships. The Germans were happy to fly with hydrogen, because they had a long history of safe, successful flights with this gas. The decision turned out to be the wrong one.

The fatal flight

The *Hindenburg* left Frankfurt, Germany for the United States on 3 May 1937. The airship flew over the Netherlands and the English Channel before heading out across the Atlantic Ocean, where strong headwinds slowed the flight. Three days later, the airship flew over the skyscrapers of New York City, and in less than an hour and a half, was ready to land at Lakehurst, New Jersey. Poor weather conditions delayed landing. Just after 7.00 p.m. the *Hindenburg* at last made its final approach to the mooring mast at Lakehurst and dropped its landing ropes.

The *Hindenburg* flies over New York City.

At 7.25 p.m. there was a muffled explosion and flames suddenly shot upwards from the rear of the airship. The fire quickly spread to the front, and the whole airship burned up in just 37 seconds. People jumped out of the windows as the frame crashed to the ground, but passengers and crew who were deep inside the ship had no chance of escape. Thirteen of the 36 passengers and 22 of the 61 crew members died, along with a member of the ground crew.

FAIL!

What caused the disaster?

We do not know for certain what caused the fire. Many theories were suggested, and most investigators believed that the fire was started by a spark of static electricity. In recent years, however, engineers have suggested that it might well have been the airship's flammable fabric covering that caused the problem. The cotton had been soaked in a cellulose-based paint that burned easily.

What has been learned?

Whatever the cause of the *Hindenburg* disaster, one thing is certain. The failure caused the end of the zeppelin passenger era. Today airships are still used for advertising, **surveillance**, **freight**, and recreational flying. Many of these are non-rigid airships, or blimps. They are filled with helium, and modern coverings are made of non-flammable synthetic materials.

Eyewitness report

Reporter Herbert Morrison described events live for the WLS radio station in Chicago:

"Here it comes, ladies and gentlemen, and what a sight it is, a thrilling one, a marvellous sight ... It burst into flames, and it's falling, it's crashing! ... This is the worst of the worst catastrophes in the world! There's smoke, and there's flames, now, and the frame is crashing to the ground ... Oh, the humanity, and all the passengers screaming around here! ... I can't talk, ladies and gentlemen".

Modern zeppelin

The successor to Count von Zeppelin's company still makes airships. Its latest model is the Zeppelin NT, a helium-filled, semi-rigid airship, with a simple internal frame made of graphite-reinforced plastic and aluminium. The frame holds the engines, steering fins, and cabin. Crew and passengers fly in the cabin beneath the balloon.

The Zeppelin NT is very different from the *Hindenburg*. It is mainly used for short tourist flights, sightseeing, and advertising, as well as for photography, television, and film shoots. It is much smaller than the 1930s craft, as the table below shows.

Other failures

There had already been other airship failures, such as the American 207-metre (679-foot) long helium-filled *Shenandoah* in 1925 and the British 237-metre (777-foot) long hydrogen-filled R101 in 1930, which killed 15 and 48 people respectively. The *Shenandoah* was on its 57th flight when it was caught in a violent storm over Ohio, USA. Turbulence tore the naval airship apart and it crashed to the ground in several pieces. Among the survivors was Chief Petty Officer Frederick Tobin who, 12 years later, was among the naval landing crew at Lakehurst when the *Hindenburg* caught fire.

	Hindenburg	Zeppelin NT
First flight	4 March 1936	18 September 1997
Crew	40-61	2
Passengers	50-72	12
Length (metres/feet)	245 (803)	75 (246)
Width (metres/feet)	41 (134.5)	19.5 (64)
Gas	Hydrogen	Helium
Volume (metres^3/feet^3)	200,000 (706,2933)	8,425 (297,526)
Top speed per hour	135 kilometres (84 miles)	125 kilometres (77 miles)

Titanic

The *Titanic* is one of the most famous passenger ships in history. It was launched to a huge fanfare and was seen as a symbol of transport technology in the early 20th century. Yet the *Titanic* was an enormous failure. People called the luxurious liner "unsinkable", but on its very first voyage across the Atlantic in 1912 the *Titanic* struck an iceberg and sank. More than 1,500 people died in the disaster. Following an inquiry, new safety rules were developed for passenger ships.

From shipyard to sea

Construction of the *Titanic* began at a shipyard in Belfast, Northern Ireland, in 1909. The **hull** was launched two years later, and the completed ship was ready for its maiden voyage from Southampton in 1912. Shortly after leaving the dock, the *Titanic's* enormous swell (high waves caused by the ship's movement) caused problems for another ocean liner and the two ships missed each other by little more than a metre. Nevertheless, all was well as the *Titanic* arrived at Cherbourg, France, and picked up more passengers. Next stop was Queenstown, Ireland, from where the ship headed out across the Atlantic Ocean.

On 10 April 1912 the *Titanic* left Southampton, bound for New York.

Who was on board?

The captain of the *Titanic*, 62-year-old Edward J. Smith, was on his last voyage before retirement. He had seven officers, who were in charge of the deck crew, engineers, stewards, restaurant staff, and musicians. There were 899 crew members on board.

There were 1,324 passengers. More than half the passengers were in cheap steerage – third-class cabins shared by up to eight people. Most steerage passengers were on a one-way ticket to the United States in search of a new life.

About a quarter of the *Titanic*'s passengers were in luxurious first-class cabins, called state rooms, on the upper and promenade decks. A smaller number were in the less expensive second class.

The iceberg

The *Titanic's* radio operators received warnings of icebergs from other ships during the crossing, but no one was worried. Then, at 11.40 p.m. on 14 April, as the ship was south-east of Newfoundland, the lookouts suddenly yelled, "Iceberg, right ahead!" It was too late to take evasive action because the ship was travelling fast, at about 39 kilometres (24 miles) per hour. The *Titanic* hit the iceberg. Though it was a glancing blow, it made cracks in the ship's steel hull. Water poured in and flooded 6 of the hull's 16 compartments. These compartments were the main reason why the ship was thought to be unsinkable, but no more than two could fail for disaster to be avoided.

Leaving the sinking ship

At 12.10 a.m., the radio operator sent a distress signal. Fifteen minutes later, the first lifeboats were loaded with women and children, and they left the ship at 12.45 a.m. Organization was poor and many of the lifeboats were not full. Ten minutes later, distress rockets were fired. The last lifeboat left the ship at 2.05 a.m., just as the **stern** of the ship rose very steeply. Fifteen minutes later, the ship broke in two and quickly sank. A nearby ship called the *Carpathia* had received the *Titanic's* distress call at 12.25 a.m. and sailed 93 kilometres (58 miles) to pick up the first lifeboat at 4.10 a.m. Another ship, the *Californian*, stopped about 32 kilometres (20 miles) from the *Titanic* because of the ice. It did not arrive until 7.30 a.m., when it was too late to rescue any survivors. The sinking resulted in the deaths of more than 1,500 of the 2,223 people on board.

This illustration of the sinking of the *Titanic* appeared in a newspaper in April 1912.

FAIL!

How did the disaster change things?

Two years later, representatives of sea-going nations met in London and adopted the International Convention for the Safety of Life at Sea (SOLAS). This was in direct response to the *Titanic* disaster. Further SOLAS measures were introduced in 1929 and 1948, and the most recent update was in 2009. The Convention also agreed to set up an International Maritime Organization, which became an agency of the United Nations, with 169 member states.

SOLAS changes

Lifeboats: Under the convention, passenger ships must carry enough lifeboats for all passengers, plus life rafts for a quarter of them. The *Titanic* lifeboats were open and gave no protection against the cold, so some passengers died of **hypothermia**. Lifeboats today have to be fully or partially enclosed. Some *Titanic* passengers jumped into the lifeboats as they were lowered, often injuring themselves or other passengers, so emergency evacuation chutes were introduced.

Lifeboat drill: No drill was held on the *Titanic*. Under SOLAS an abandon-ship drill and fire drill must take place weekly on all passenger ships.

Immersion suits: Many *Titanic* passengers died in the freezing sea. Under SOLAS, a number of immersion suits, which protect the wearer from hypothermia, must be carried on board ships.

The lifeboats issue

Titanic had a total of 20 lifeboats with room for 1,186 people – just over half the number of people on board. This was the main reason that less than a third of the total number of crew and passengers survived. Those who were left behind and jumped into the sea quickly froze to death in the icy water.

Public address (PA) system: There was no PA system on the *Titanic* and news reached passengers slowly, adding to the confusion and panic. Today, PAs are a requirement.

Distress alert: The *Titanic's* radio had a range of 200 nautical miles. This was increased, and ships can now communicate globally via satellites. Also, the land station at Newfoundland received *Titanic's* distress call but the airwaves were crackling and the ship's position was misinterpreted. Today, with a global positioning system, a ship's position is sent automatically. Every ship at sea must maintain a continuous watch on the distress frequencies.

Ice patrol: After the *Titanic* disaster, ice patrols were set up in the north Atlantic and are still a requirement. When ice is reported near a ship's course at night, the ship must proceed at a moderate speed or alter course.

"The age of the mega-ship is clearly upon us ... Ships should be designed with increased survivability so that in the event of [an accident], passengers can stay safely onboard as the ship proceeds to port."

World Cruise Industry Review, 2008

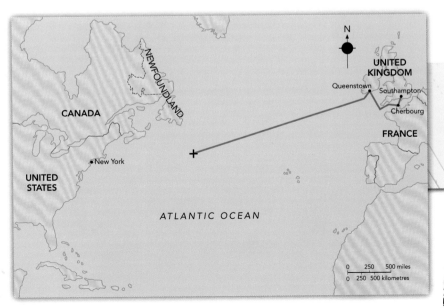

This map shows the route taken by the *Titanic* on her one and only voyage.

Bigger and bigger

Today's biggest passenger ships are even larger than the *Titanic*. The table below compares the *Titanic* to a modern ocean liner.

	Titanic	Oasis of the Seas
Capacity (tonnes/tons)	42 029 (46,329)	204 372 (225,282)
Length (metres/feet)	269 (882)	360 (1,181)
Width at widest point (metres/feet)	28 (91.8)	47 (154)
Decks	10	18
Speed (kilometres per hour/miles per hour)	43 (27)	42 (26)
Passengers and crew	3,547	8,461
Year of maiden voyage	1912	2009

The enormous *Oasis of the Seas* ocean liner was launched in 2009 in Finland. The ship's maiden voyage was to the United States.

What has been learned?

Whatever the regulations, if a ship is overcrowded, there will be problems in the event of an accident. In 1987 a Philippine ferry, the *Doña Paz*, collided with another ship, caught fire, and sank. The ship had a capacity of 1,518 passengers, and the official number of dead is listed as 1,840. Unofficial sources say that more than 4,000 people lost their lives in the accident. There was no time to lower lifeboats before the sinking, but there would never have been enough for the extra passengers anyway. Although we have learned a great deal from the *Titanic* disaster, there is still room for improvement in safety on the seas.

Worried friends and relatives check a list of the passengers on board the *Doña Paz* ferry after it sank in 1987.

Ro-ro problems

The *Titanic* was thought to be unsinkable because of its bulkheads (upright walls in the hull that created separate compartments). Roll-on/roll-off (or ro-ro) ferries have few bulkheads and this has caused problems. Ro-ros are designed to carry cars and lorries, which can "roll on" and "roll off" the ship in port. They have large external doors close to the waterline, and open vehicle decks. This has given them a reputation for being a high-risk design, especially since 1987, when an open loading door caused the *Herald of Free Enterprise* ferry to capsize.

Timeline

1492   Leonardo da Vinci designs and draws flying machines

1769   First self-propelled road vehicle invented by Nicolas-Joseph Cugnot. James Watt **patents** his improved steam engine.

1783   French brothers Jacques Étienne and Joseph-Michel Montgolfier launch the first hot-air passenger balloons

1814   English engineer George Stephenson builds the first practical steam-powered railway locomotive

1853   George Cayley builds the first heavier-than-air aircraft, a glider

1885   German engineer Karl Benz builds a three-wheeled automobile with an internal-combustion engine

1897   German engineer Rudolf Diesel invents the diesel engine. American twins Francis and Freelan Stanley build their first Steamer car.

1900   Ferdinand von Zeppelin's first airship, the LZ-1, makes its first flight

1903   On 8 December, Samuel Langley's Aerodrome aircraft fails. On 17 December, the Wright Brothers fly the world's first power-driven aeroplane.

1908   American Henry Ford produces the Model T car, selling 15 million over the next twenty years

1912   The *Titanic* sinks on her maiden voyage. US designer Glenn Curtiss demonstrates the first successful flying boat, the *Flying Fish*.

1933   American inventor Buckminster Fuller introduces his Dymaxion car, which fails

1935   Howard Hughes sets a new speed record of 568 kph (353 mph) in his H-1 racing plane

1937   German airship *Hindenburg* bursts into flames in
        New Jersey

1947   US Air Force Major Charles Yeager breaks the sound
        barrier in a Bell X-1. Howard Hughes takes off briefly in
        his Hercules H-4 (Spruce Goose).

1954   Boeing 707 jet airliner makes its first flight. USS *Nautilus*
        is the first nuclear-powered submarine.

1958   Ford introduces the Nucleon nuclear-powered concept car

1961   **Soviet** cosmonaut Yuri Gagarin is the first man in space

1962   Bell Aircraft Corporation develops its jet pack

1967   US *Apollo 1* fails on the launch pad. Soviet Soyuz 1
        crash-lands.

1968   Tupolev Tu-144 makes its first flight

1969   First flight of the Boeing 747, the first commercial
        wide-body jumbo jet. First manned Moon landing by
        Apollo 11. First flight of Concorde.

1973   The Mizar flying car is launched and fails

1981   First flight of the US space shuttle. France begins
        operating its TGV (high-speed train).

1984   NASA's Manned Maneuvering Unit is used on three
        space missions

1985   Sinclair C5 electric vehicle is launched

1986   Space shuttle *Challenger*, with seven people on board,
        explodes after lift-off

1987   Philippine ferry *Doña Paz* sinks. British ro-ro ferry *Herald
        of Free Enterprise* capsizes.

2009   Volkswagen unveil their electric E-Up car. Aptera unveil
        their 2e electric car. Terrafugia test-fly their Transition
        roadable aircraft.

Glossary

aeronautics study and practice of making and flying aircraft

atmosphere layer of gases that surrounds Earth

biofuel fuel produced from plant or animal matter

enterprise ability to undertake bold or difficult projects

fibreglass plastic material reinforced with glass fibres

flammable something that catches fire easily

freight goods that are transported; cargo

hull body of a ship

hypothermia extremely low body temperature, which can lead to death

Industrial Revolution when Britain and other countries were transformed from agricultural into industrial nations in the 18th and 19th centuries

monoplane aeroplane with one pair of wings

nucleus (*plural* **nuclei**) central part of an atom (the smallest part of a chemical element)

patent exclusive right of an inventor to make and sell an invention

propaganda misleading publicity for a cause or point of view

propulsion force of driving something forwards or making it work

prototype first example of something new, such as the first of a new type of aircraft

radioactive decaying plutonium or uranium that can be harmful to humans exposed to it

reactor device in which nuclear reactions take place to produce power

shock waves sharp changes in air pressure

sonic boom loud noise caused by the shock wave from an aircraft travelling faster than the speed of sound

Soviet of the Soviet Union, another name for the USSR

stern back end of a ship or submarine

supersonic faster than the speed of sound, which varies from about 1,060 kilometres (659 miles) per hour to 1,225 kilometres (761 miles) per hour depending on the temperature of the air

surveillance close observation, often of enemies, suspected spies, or criminals

thrust force of forward movement

USSR Union of Soviet Socialist Republics, also known as the Soviet Union. The communist state that existed from 1922 to 1991, including Russia and 14 other republics.

Find out more

Books and films

A *Century of Manned Flight*, Richard Bickers (Bramley Books, 1998)

Concorde: A Photographic History, Jonathan Falconer (Haynes, 2008)

Eyewitness: Titanic, Simon Adams (Dorling Kindersley, 2004)

Man, Moment, Machine: Howard Hughes and the Spruce Goose (The History Channel, A & E Home Video, 2007)

When Disaster Struck: The Hindenburg 1937, Jane Bingham (Raintree, 2006)

Websites

www.nasa.gov/mission_pages/apollo/missions/apollo1.html
Have a look at the NASA website to find out more information about Apollo 1 and other past missions.

www.bbc.co.uk/archive/titanic
This BBC website has lots of information about the construction and sinking of the *Titanic*.

www.britishairways.com/concorde/index.html
Find out everything there is to know about Concorde on this website.

Further research

Here are some more transport topics to research:

- The Montgolfier brothers, Joseph-Michel (1740–1810) and Jacques Étienne (1745–99): in 1783 the brothers sent the first manned hot-air balloon into the skies above Paris.

- George Cayley (1773–1857): this British engineer and inventor built the first successful man-carrying glider. On the first flight of his *New Flyer* in 1853, Cayley's coachman flew for 450 metres (1,476 feet), and then cried, "Please, Sir George, I wish to give notice. I was hired to drive and not to fly!"

- Otto Lilienthal (1848–1896): a German engineer, Lilienthal made more than 2,000 flights with his own gliders. He was killed when one of his aircraft crashed into a hillside.

- Hubert Latham (1883–1912): a rival of Louis Blériot (1872–1936), who made the first international flight, from England to France, in 1909. Latham was much less well known than Blériot, even though he broke speed and altitude records.

Index